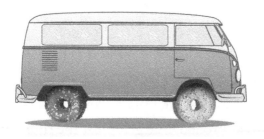

PRAISE FOR
THIS BOOK

Reading this book is just like you're actually talking with Beth. You can hear her speaking to you throughout the story. As she says in the introduction, there's good and bad, happy and sad, but a drive forward the entire time.

I'm one of those people who ask, "Why not?" instead of "Why?" I had more unique experiences at A Little Something Bakery than I ever would have thought possible. And how could I not help out? Such great people.

Dave Simonson

The author takes us on a very personal and honest journey. She does an excellent job at getting to the "WHY" and "HOW" of starting or rejuvenating a business in a plain, simple, and straightforward approach. She gives just the right amount of homework with the available worksheets. She uses her easy-to-get-to-know demeanor to guide an entrepreneur in realizing their potential.

As you read, you will feel like you know Beth as a neighbor and friend. The author lets us see her strengths and weaknesses through real-life examples of what worked for her. She allows us to meet the most influential people in her life. I enjoyed seeing how these individuals molded the way she ran her business. They all made her the trusted entrepreneur that she is today.

I loved going down memory lane with A Little Something Bakery. The examples of how patrons became family are real. She gives these examples for a reason. The network of patrons/family that she built over the years served as her best support during the ups and downs of this and any business. Beth has determination and a never-give-up attitude. She may get knocked down, but she finds a way to get back up again with grace.

This book will help get any first-time business owner or any business needing a boost to the next level. She may not share her recipe for the "Dirtbombs," but she will share the invaluable knowledge that she gained through times of feast and famine.

Amy Kidd

In this book, Beth describes how difficult and emotional being an entrepreneur is and how many unforeseen circumstances can set any business down a path they wish not to go. Beth speaks directly to the reader to make them feel comfortable about the process, be prepared with the tools they need to start off right and understand the importance of doing your research.

Beth Bolton was a light to the dark halls of 485 New Park Avenue. Her laughter, spirit, and kindness are like a magnet for me. I admire Beth's strength and determination above anything else.

She has been through the wringer and back, and she keeps moving forward with that smile, a little sarcasm, and a healthy amount of pride.

Beth's new path to help others succeed in business is a natural fit since she has been in business for over 30 years. She has helped me make some major business decisions of my own. Beth has given me the motivation to strive for more and see the things in myself I wasn't so sure existed.

Jennifer O'Connell

FOR THE L♥VE OF CAKE

FOR THE L♥VE OF CAKE

An Entrepreneur's Journey

BETH BOLTON

ACADEMY
PRESS

For permission requests, write to the below address:

Beth Bolton
430 New Park Avenue, Suite 102
West Hartford, CT 06110

The opinions expressed by the Author are not necessarily those held by PYP Academy Press.

Ordering Information: Quantity sales and special discounts are available on quantity purchases by corporations, associations, and others. For details, contact the author at beth@bethbolton.com.

Edited by: Nancy Graham-Tillman
Cover design by: Nelly Murariu
Back cover by: Marlene Kurban
Typeset by: Medlar Publishing Solutions Pvt Ltd., India

Printed in the United States of America.

ISBN: 978-1-951591-67-0 (paperback)
ISBN: 978-1-951591-68-7 (hardcover)
ISBN: 978-1-951591-69-4 (ebook)

Library of Congress Control Number: 2021911584

First edition, July 2021

The information contained within this book is strictly for informational purposes. The material may include information, products, or services by third parties. As such, the Author and Publisher do not assume responsibility or liability for any third-party material or opinions. The publisher is not responsible for websites (or their content) that are not owned by the publisher. Readers are advised to do their own due diligence when it comes to making decisions.

The mission of the Publish Your Purpose Academy Press is to discover and publish authors who are striving to make a difference in the world. We give underrepresented voices power and a stage to share their stories, speak their truth, and impact their communities. Do you have a book idea you would like us to consider publishing? Please visit PublishYourPurposePress.com for more information.

 PYP Academy Press
141 Weston Street, #155
Hartford, CT, 06141

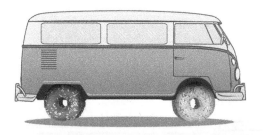

DISCLAIMER

The information provided within this book is for general informational and educational purposes only. The author makes no representations or warranties, expressed or implied, about the completeness, accuracy, reliability, suitability, or availability with respect to the information, products, services, or related graphics contained in this book for any purpose. Any use of this information is at your own risk.

The advice and strategies found within may not be suitable for every situation. This work is sold with the understanding that neither the author nor the publisher is held responsible for the results accrued from the advice in this book.

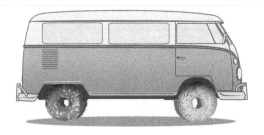

DEDICATION

To my husband, Tony Bolton, of 35 years.
He has walked each and every step of this
journey with me. I could not have done it
without him. I am very grateful for his love and
support, along with his blood, sweat, and tears.
He is my foundation and my best friend.
I love you!
THE AWESOME TONY BOLTON
ROLL TIDE ROLL

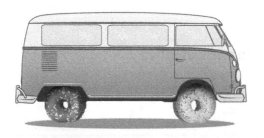

TABLE OF CONTENTS

SECTION 1
LET'S STOP AT
A LITTLE SOMETHING BAKERY

SECTION 2
INGREDIENTS NEEDED FOR
A SUCCESSFUL SMALL BUSINESS

Table of Contents

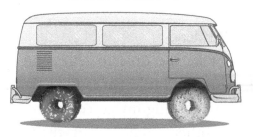

LET'S STOP AT A LITTLE SOMETHING BAKERY

A LETTER FROM THE AUTHOR

Dear Readers,

As I take the time to reflect on the process of closing A Little Something Bakery after 11 years and turning my career in the direction of helping other women start their journeys, I've been looking back at some of the things I've learned the hard way. I lived through these misfortunes and would not give up. Not sure if I was strong-willed or bullheaded for not throwing in the towel.

Quitting wasn't an option—that voice kept telling me to keep going.

When I speak about running my own business and encourage others to do so, I like to use the analogy that you are the "bus driver" of your dream. There is a road map that you need to be very familiar with before you start off on your journey. You'll need certain people to help you get your destination, but you'll also need a strong framework for your bus. As you start off, you must have all the necessary items packed for your trip. You'll pick up your riders as you go, and each rider will play an intricate roll along your path. The riders will change from time to time; you may even have to kick some of them off the bus. No worries, your road map will help you change a few things around so you can keep moving forward.

Many misfortunes (as I like to call them) can happen along the way. Some of them are completely out of your control and some of these misfortunes happen when you make a wrong turn. If you make that wrong turn, there is time to change your course and get back on the road. Hopefully, you haven't gotten too far-off track.

I want to help all women who aim to be their own bus driver by assisting them in finding the know-how to make the right decisions and putting them into action so they can bring their dreams to life. It's my sincere hope that in focusing on this next chapter in my career, I can help other women business owners avoid the misfortunes I've suffered so that their bus remains a strong, well-oiled machine.

In this book, I'll show you how to drive your own bus. We're going on a journey together.

I'll take you through what it's like to own your own business. My journey will show you the good: how much I loved my shop and all the love I shared with the people who came in. It will also show you the bad and the ugly–and let me tell you, there was both.

This book will teach you about a business plan using no big fancy words, just plain and simple terms.

Along our journey, we will:

- Talk about what you want to achieve (your "WHAT")
- Investigate your vision statement (your "WHY")
- Construct a mission statement (your "HOW")
- Determine who your customer is and get to know them (your "WHO")
- Make sure you understand and know who your competitor is (your "COMPETITION")
- Ensure you know where you are going (your "WHERE")
- Discuss other aspects of your plan.

Photo by Nicole Bedard

I'll make sure you understand the importance of taking the steps needed for building a strong foundation. You are the bus driver on your journey; you sit in that driver's seat and drive your bus to where it needs to go. I'll be the guide who will prepare you for how your journey will be.

I'm so passionate about this book because not only do I get to show you the joy and happiness that was created within our community, but I also get to prepare you for everything that will jump out in front of you while you're driving your own bus. This book should make you laugh, it might make you cry, and it will for sure educate. If opening a small business is your goal, then you're in the right place.

I'll be with you every step of the way. And if you hit a rough patch and need me to drive, then I'll be there to take the wheel. I'll help you get to where you are going. What path are you going to use to get there? What will *your* bus look like?

I have my new bus; her name is WANDA. She came to me while I was preparing for this journey. She is a vintage VW bus, but I think I'm older than she is! Wanda is not too big; she has just enough room to carry everything I need. The seats are comfortable, and the ride is smooth. My first bus was a mom, three-seat-in-the-back station wagon. She was a pretty shade of green with a tan interior. (Not sure why I got one with tan interior; it didn't stay tan for very long.) She hauled the neighborhood kids to school, picked up ingredients when needed, and delivered a LOT of cake to wherever it needed to go. She took some wrong turns sometimes, but we were always able to get ourselves back to where we needed to be.

I ask you to have a seat on my bus as we take the journey through my bakery years.

Keep your eyes open, there's a lot to see.

Beth Bolton

CHAPTER 1

MY BAKERY

A Little Something Bakery
335 Park Road
West Hartford, CT

I opened A Little Something Bakery in February of 2009. I loved everything about my bakery; it was my dream come true. The bakery sat on one of the busiest corners in my town. I loved watching people walking by and stopping to look in the windows. From the inside I could see everything going on outside, and I watched as cars stopped at the traffic light that was right on the corner in front of us.

335 Park Road is a historical and quaint part of West Hartford. Long before A Little Something Bakery made 335 Park Road its home, the location housed a TV repair shop, then added an estate jewelry store, and later an extension of a mom-and-pop grocery store.

When you walked into the bakery, the wood on the front door squeaked, as did the original hardwood floors in certain spots. All the walls were painted a cream color, and the ceiling and trim were dark green. It was a little masculine for my liking, so I painted it pink, kept the green trim, and gussied it up with floral prints and white curtains. As you looked straight ahead and

to your right, you could see the display cases full of all kinds of deliciousness.

The shop had that sweet buttery smell; you could just close your eyes, inhale, and remember that smell. You could walk right up to the counter and see everything right in front of you: rows of cupcakes, morning treats, and cookies in their jars. Children would place their faces right up to the glass case to get that closer look. We had an open kitchen so you could always see what we were making and taking out of the ovens.

A Little Something Bakery grew busy very fast. It seemed people just couldn't get enough our treats. They would line up on Saturday mornings for scones, muffins, coffeecake, and "Dirtbombs." Dirtbombs were baked like a muffin and tasted like an old-fashioned donut. When they came out of the oven, they were immediately dipped in melted butter and then rolled in a cinnamon/sugar mixture. Everything was made like Grandma would make them with butter, sugar, flour, milk, and eggs. You were able to understand every ingredient we used— no preservatives added. Nothing fancy, but oh so good.

The shop had a way of transporting people to happy times. It was like coming home from school and smelling chocolate chip cookies fresh out of the oven or breathing in the smell of Grandma's pies during the holiday season. For me, it reminded me of walking through the back door of my friend Nancy's house. Her mom, Anna Fournier, would have some just-baked Blondies. We would sit at the kitchen table and eat those scrumptious treats with a glass of milk, and we were good to go until supper time.

The day of Mrs. Fournier's funeral, I walked through the back door of her home as I had done a thousand times before. I brought a platter of treats for the gathering. As I walked into the darkened dining room, I placed the platter on the table. I instantly became frozen in time standing there. I was catapulted back 40 years walking into that kitchen after school. Mrs. Fournier was always in the kitchen it seemed. She was making dinner, baking, doing the dishes. I stood there wondering where that sweet buttery smell went. I couldn't smell it. And where was Mrs. Fournier? I didn't see her. Mr. Fournier, Joe, was nowhere to be found either. Mr. Fournier was always in the living room. (I'm pretty sure I annoyed the shit out of that man as a teenager. I loved to talk to him, but he was not a man of many words.) I came back to the kitchen and cried like a baby. It was a loss so different than I had experienced before. Not just because the world lost a beautiful human being, but because I knew it wouldn't be the same walking through that back door ever again. Was I being selfish? I didn't care. Anna Fournier was one special woman, and I wanted to remember her in that kitchen.

Nancy had sent me a Christmas card that year. Inside was a handwritten card with the blondie recipe on it—a gift that I'll always treasure. It felt like I could hold a small part of Mrs. Fournier and keep her close. We made those blondies in my shop and they were a big seller.

A Little Something Bakery was that kind of place; it was like that special kitchen. The bakery had a way of wrapping its arms around you like a well-worn blanket. The smiles and laughter were amazing. It was a place you could bring your children and feel at ease. It made you feel like you were sitting in your own kitchen.

We met some of the nicest, sweetest, quirkiest people you would ever want to meet, and they became our treasured family and friends for years to come. Our community was the best, and they were so welcoming. I was overwhelmed at how well received we were. This community was a mixture of young and old. There were lots of kids and mommies with babies in strollers, and a lot of dogs and dog walkers came by. Members of our police and fire department as well as our animal control officer all made sure to stop in. The actors and staff at The Playhouse on Park would also come in. I've stayed in touch with many of them. I couldn't have asked for a better community.

CHAPTER

OUR COMMUNITY

It really was more than a bakery; this was a community collaboration that helped nurture our kids. Funny thing: when anyone said, "the bakery," people knew exactly where you meant. When I said "Beth" (no last name required), the person or people I was talking to knew exactly who I was talking about.
— Sabina Maria

Inside our small shop, we served as a spot for people to start their day off, meet and mingle, sneak away from work to get that little afternoon pick me up, or grab that dessert for after supper.

We also became a spot that was about family. Rosemary had lost her husband, Al. I loved this couple so much. They lived in my neighborhood, and my children called them Grandma and Grandpa. After Al passed away, Rosemary would come in and scoop cookies for us on Tuesday mornings. The girls would make the batter and Rosemary would scoop the cookies. It really had less to do with scooping cookies and more to do with nurturing a companionship that grew into love. A Little Something Bakery is where Rosemary did some of her grieving. I'm so glad that we could help her through a rough patch.

Then there were people like Tracey Gamer-Fanning and Mike Keo, who shared their engagements with us while it was happening, it was so exciting. We were later invited to be part of both of their big days and designed their wedding cakes.

Oh, and the small children we watched grow. How could Elizabeth, Aiden, Eleanor,

Avery, Patrick, and all the others grow up so fast right in front of our eyes? And couples we made wedding cakes for were now back for a baby shower cake, a christening cake, and OMG, the first-year birthday cake. It was amazing to me how many people became part of our big family.

It didn't take long for our immediate community to grow. We were there to help our local schools, places of worship, sports teams, and other local businesses. After realizing I couldn't help everybody, I chose to help the three organizations that were near and dear to my heart. I focused on our two high school Safe Grad events, our local American Cancer Society's Relay for Life Walk, and last but certainly not least, our local Autism Speaks chapter.

1. Safe Grad is a 30^+ year tradition in our town's two high schools. It's an all-night, post-graduation, drug- and alcohol-free celebration that brings seniors together for one last memorable event. The event is funded by parents, community members, and local businesses. It was a way I could give back to

the schools that my children attended. I'm just glad I didn't raise my hand to be a parent who stayed all night!

2. American Cancer Society's Relay for Life is a special event. Many communities across this country have heard of this event. I don't know of anybody who hasn't been touched by cancer. This event is to honor and memorialize them and make us stop for an evening and realize how grateful we should be for the medical advances for cancer. I donated the desserts for "The Survivor Dinner." We picked up the meal that was donated from a local restaurant, brought it to the event space, and helped set it up. The dinner was a special way to celebrate those who have made it.

I always stayed for the luminaria ceremony. It's a very humbling part of the event when luminarias are dedicated to a loved one lost, someone currently battling cancer, or someone who has overcome it. The luminarias are lit right after sunset in remembrance of a life touched by cancer. Attendees remain silent so they can hear every name read for whom a luminaria was lit. I don't know if I'll ever see cancer eradicated in my lifetime, but I sure do hope that progress keeps moving forward.

3. Autism Speaks is committed to finding a cure for autism through advocacy and support. Through dedicated funding, the organization helps advance research efforts that examine the causes, preventions, and treatments for autism. Autism Speaks strives to increase awareness about autism spectrum disorders and advocates for the needs of individuals with autism and their families.

The following is an excerpt from an article written about my bakery's support of Autism Speaks: April 2012

A Little Something Bakery is Giving a Little Something Back: West Hartford bakery will donate a portion of sales of special 'Puzzle Piece' cookies to Autism Speaks.
– Ronni Newton, Patch Staff

In recognition of the continually growing community support it enjoys, A Little Something Bakery is giving a little something back to the community. A portion of the proceeds of each of its Puzzle Piece Cookies sold throughout April will go to Autism Speaks, the nation's largest autism science and advocacy organization.

April is Autism Awareness Month. The bakery's popular Puzzle Piece Cookies resemble the Autism Speaks logo.

"Autism Speaks is a wonderful organization that does so much for so many people, and we're proud to do our little part to support their efforts," says Beth Bolton, owner of the company that has a growing reputation as West Hartford's premier neighborhood bakery. "If enough of us support their work, maybe we'll get closer to solving the riddle and the puzzle of autism."

Giving back to your community is a fulfilling feeling of contributing to your neighbors. It's a wonderful way to get to know the people who

live, work, or shop in your community. You get the opportunity to meet many new people and broaden your network. Giving back will help you understand the circumstances others face in your community. Having an open-minded perspective of different walks of life will help you be an empathetic and effective member of the community.

BUILDING
A GOOD TEAM

*We do not create a team just
to work together. We have a team because
we respect, trust, and care for one another.*
– Anonymous

As we were finding our way and making our presence felt within the community, I realized that we would need to hire some people to help us. I had some of the most amazing people work for me in my shop.

First, I started out with my husband, Tony; my son, Christopher; and my daughter, Sarah. My sister, Karen, and my niece, Allison, were the next two. As we kept growing, our need for counter help increased. I had many angel hands who came in to help me, each providing assistance when they could. I have two other nieces who live nearby who spent time with me. Nicole and Rachael are sisters, and they were with me through their high school years and some of college also. These three young ladies basically recruited the rest of my front-of-house staff. I asked them if they had a friend who would like a job at the bakery, which gave the girls pride and ownership. Almost all the girls had extracurricular activities, so I made it their responsibility to make sure there was coverage and keep me informed if we were having a problem. They were usually good at keeping everything on track.

I had many women who worked for me in all aspects of the bakery: Nancy, Ashley, Crystal, Liana, Kasey, Lauren, and a few more. They did their jobs well, but in hindsight I would have changed some things. I would have made sure each baker signed a non-disclosure agreement. I would have also made sure I was very precise in defining their job descriptions and included those in their contracts. I didn't hire many people, so I thought that it wasn't necessary; but in fact, it doesn't matter how many employees you have. To ensure you have a good team in place, everybody needs to know exactly what their job description is and what they need to be held accountable for.

At A Little Something Bakery, these young ladies and women were my front-seat riders on my bus. This is how special they thought A Little Something Bakery was:

"A ride to work? Absolutely not. I woke up just before sunrise on a Saturday morning to walk to one of my many opening shifts. First, I unlock the back door, turn on the lights, and make my way to the double-doored steel oven, setting it to 350. The anticipatory smell of blueberry muffins and freshly ground coffee

were two of many small perks that made my time at A Little Something Bakery so enjoyable.

I applied to work at the bakery when I was 16 years old. And like any teenager, I was in hopes of earning some extra money. About six years later, I gained much more than I'd asked for. The family-owned business located just around the corner from my childhood home provided me with my first employment experience that laid the foundation for many skills I exercise several years later. I learned how to use a cash register, power-wash a cookie sheet, and increase my calorie intake with little-to-no regrets—a mindset that seemingly followed me into adulthood.

In the simplest terms, my first job (ironically) taught me how to work. But this was more than that. A Little Something Bakery taught me how to enjoy what I do and how to walk into a space and acknowledge my responsibilities with great pleasure. Beth Bolton gave me more than just employment *experience, she provided me with a small space on the corner of Park and South Quaker to explore my creativity and most importantly, feel like I was part of the family.*

The smell of freshly baked blueberry muffins on a dewy Saturday morning was a reminder of the endless love poured into every corner of that building. From late-night giggle sessions with Beth and peers over excess buttercream frosting, to the kaleidoscope-colored sprinkles that danced over freshly frosted Funfetti cupcakes, these memories leave me feeling grateful. Not only for the experience, but also for the person who gave me a chance, taught me more than I could ever explain, and watched me grow into the woman I am today. For that I am forever thankful to have experienced the pure love that Beth extended not only to her delicious treats, but to everyone around her.

To the entire Bolton & A Little Something family that helped to manifest my sweet sanctuary, thank you."

Shannon Griffith

Shannon is an amazing young woman who I fell in love with the moment I met her. She's quiet, but when she has something to say you want to stop and listen. I'm the lucky one to have met Shannon and to have her and her mom, Sabina, in our lives.

"They say the sense of smell can transport you back in time. I can attest to that. I grew up in West Hartford, Connecticut, the daughter of a woman who loved to bake. Every Saturday morning my brother and I would wake to the aroma of a delicious treat baking in the oven. We would race downstairs and lurk in the kitchen waiting for the prized chocolate-covered spatula; the winner forfeiting any claim to the mixing bowl. It didn't take much to make us happy—a mouthful of chocolate and we were on our way. Equipped with my mother's mixing bowls and measuring cups (my most prized possessions), this was a tradition I carried on with my own children.

From the very first moment I stepped into A Little Something Bakery, newly hired by my friend, the owner, I knew I was in a place whose business was that of making memories. Not only did I recall forgotten memories of my own, but I was also privileged to play a part in the memory-making of others.

Most celebrations end with a dessert, be it a child's birthday party, a wedding, or a retirement party. All those occasions create memories we carry with us our entire lifetime. A Little Something Bakery wasn't only Beth's dream; it was where a bride's dream of the perfect wedding cake, a child's favorite character, or a retiree's hobby came to life. The amazingly talented artists I worked with made dreams come true and created memories.

I have so many wonderful memories of working at A Little Something Bakery. Suffice it to say, we all need A Little Something."

Nancy McCabe-Sullivan

My dear friend Nancy has remarried and moved to the upper part of Maine, just a sneeze away from Canada. Nancy and her new husband,

Jerry, have a home and are starting a new life. I wish them nothing but peace and happiness. I'll take the six-hour drive up to see them soon.

"Working at A little Something Bakery was truly one of the highlights of my high school experience. While other friends of mine dreaded going to work, I picked up as many shifts as I could because I loved being there so much! My favorite shifts were when I came in at 6 a.m. to help with Saturday morning opening shift, but nothing could beat when you and I would close together just the two of us on a weekday, and I would fill you in on all of my high school drama. It was so nice to have a boss who cared so much about my success outside of work and my personal life. I truly thought of you as a second mom!

My favorite treats were the Elvis cupcakes, the Dirtbombs, and the caramel apple cheesecake bars. My mouth is watering just typing this! My favorite thing to do was decorate the cupcakes both for the regular counter and special orders. I still take pride in being a good baker from working there, and I credit it all to you!

Most of all though, when I think about working at the bakery, I think about the constant laughter we all shared. It was such an amazing group of girls to work with, and it's hard to remember a time where we weren't smiling and cracking each other up in between customers coming in.

I hope you are doing well, and I wish you the best of luck with everything!"

Kendall Edwards

As Kendall's boss, I watched her grow as she moved from high school onto college. She has an absolutely amazing voice, and to see the pictures of how happy she is and the places she has been just warms my heart.

As you can see, we were a special place to work. Everybody was near and dear to my heart, but I had two people who just rose to the occasion every time. They were hardworking, came to work on time, and were an absolute joy to work with.

First there was my niece, Allison Reis Castro. She came to work for me when she was about 16, and she stayed with me through her high school years, then through college, and even after she found a job teaching (second grade, God bless her). She moved with me to my new spot. I designed her wedding cake and the wedding cakes for her friends. Allison is the cutest thing; she looks just like my sister, Karen. She has the complexion of her Portuguese heritage, with the prettiest dark brown hair. She has a vibrant personality, and she came in and out of the bakery until a little after she was married.

Like all my other girls, Allison started out working the front counter. She then moved on to frosting cupcakes, and soon I started to teach her to bake. She had it in her genes; her mom is a great baker. Allison caught on to baking very quickly. She became an excellent baker, but she came in like a wrecking ball. There was flour everywhere, and if she used cocoa powder, damn! You just couldn't get mad at her though. She would clean it all up, and off she would go, leaving Uncle Tony to do the floor (ha-ha!).

And oh, how she described a "Dirtbomb" to a customer—it was epic. She stood tall and proud (at 5'2") and said that it was a corn muffin that we baked, and that when it came out of the oven, we dipped it in melted butter and then rolled it in cinnamon and sugar. I just stood there laughing under my breath until the customer left, then almost peed my pants laughing. She had everything right except it wasn't a corn muffin, but rather a batter that tasted like an old-fashioned cake donut. So funny!

Allison was standing right there next to me the first time I got my hand caught in the 20-quart mixer. She was like, "Aunt Beth, what do we do?!" I said, "Just get me some ice and call Uncle Tony to come get me." It's a good thing that my thumb on my right hand is still attached; that beater just snapped the spatula and took my thumb right with it. Yeah, it hurt. Okay, it hurt a lot, but all was well.

We shouldn't even mention the blueberry pie (LOL!). One minute Allison was holding it, next minute it was upside down on the floor, blueberry filling everywhere. The look on her face was beyond priceless as we stood there laughing.

Allison Reis Castro

I so enjoyed having Allison with me. I think I was her trusted soul. When she came in on a Saturday or Sunday morning, I got to hear the lowdown on everything that happened in school. I thought high school was active, but oh no—college, the tooth, losing her wallet, the car rolling down the driveway, the boyfriend, the girlfriends—it was like she was coming to confessional. I enjoyed all the time I spent with her. She, like my kids and my other nieces, worked so hard in college and all of them did very well in school and have excellent jobs today. I would like to think that I played a tiny part in their teenage and early adult lives with them working for me. I love them all very much and will always cherish those bakery moments.

The second person who rose to every occasion is Kerry Michael Lord. I could babble on and on for a long time about Kerry; he has been a part of our lives for six years or so. He holds an incredibly special place in my heart. He's like that little kid you just can't say no to. Kerry is a soft-spoken person and keeps very much to himself. He's resourceful and has a dry sense of humor. If he has something to say, you need to pay attention. And he can get so fired up from reading the local town news, especially when talking about politics. He gets so incredibility consumed by the topic. It's comical watching the veins start popping out of his forehead when he really gets passionate about what he's talking about.

Kerry loves music and playing video games. I love sitting and listening to him play his acoustic guitar. He becomes so calm; a peacefulness comes over him when he's playing. (And he's really good too.) Kerry's other love is working on his model trains and miniature houses. His eye for detail makes the houses and scenery look lifelike.

Even though he would never admit it, Kerry is also a master gardener—his vegetable garden looks better than anything Martha Stewart could do. The rows are perfect, and the plants look healthy and strong. Owning his own home, Kerry has a huge garden in his backyard where he loves working outside and getting his hands dirty. He's such a "proud papa" when something is ready to harvest.

Back in the '80s, Kerry lived on Quaker Lane in the Elmwood neighborhood. That was his stomping grounds along with the woods behind their house along Trout Brook. He loves his Elmwood roots, and the fact that he has lived in the same zip code for nearly his entire life says something about our community. Many of us have lived in Elmwood for most of our lives, and I don't think we would have it any other way. Kerry would always say, "Nothing good happens outside of 06110," and many of us share his feelings. This part of town is where I live and where I have spent a good portion of my life. It's where I gave my bakery a home.

Kerry came to work with me in my shop one day in April of 2016. By then, I was at my 485 New Park Avenue location. I needed some help with making little guitars on some decorated "Nurses Rock" cookies, 400 to be exact. Since he has an amazing attention to detail, I was pretty confident that his guitars would look better than mine, and of course they were. We did that order again the next year. After we got through that big project, I asked him if he would like to help me with another one. One project turned into another, and he ended up working with me on decorating cakes. By 2016, we were primarily doing custom cakes. There were things that I wasn't proficient at when it came to buttercream, but I knew that Kerry could accomplish it in fondant. His fondant work was as incredible as everything else he did. Everybody raved at how wonderful their cakes looked and how incredible they tasted. So, our partnership began; I baked, and he decorated.

We became crazy busy with our cakes. Depending on the decorations that were going on, we averaged about 15 cakes per weekend. We never turned down doing a Unicorn cake though, those were one of our favorite cakes to make; they each had their own personality. And let's not forget the cupcakes and cookies that needed to be done. Plus, we had wedding deliveries every weekend from mid-March to the end of the year. I didn't want anybody to deliver the wedding cakes but me. It was part of who I was. I had to make sure I was there to set up the cake and make it look as beautiful as the couple and I expected it to be. My husband helped me most times, but there were times when my children or a trusted friend helped me out. Inevitably, at least one time a year we were completely overbooked, so my family belonged to me that day. Each person had a delivery in a different part of the state, and they all knew what they needed to do. As I think back now, I wonder how we ever did it.

Kerry became an integral part of this organized chaos. He was masterful at his craft, and it didn't take him long to catch on to what needed to be done. He took on each project giving it a little twist of his own. Kerry was part of the reason we were so busy all the time. He never missed a single twinkle in the eye of any character on the cakes. Kerry also helped with making and decorating the cookies, and we had some great creations.

I really have to say, that period of time was when I was the happiest in my business. I had a solid foundation and a good team in place. We were busy, we were good at what we did, and everybody knew it.

At the beginning of each week, Kerry and I mapped out what needed to be done. He had his work and I had mine. We worked very well together. Tuesday through Friday the radio (105.9) belonged to Kerry, Saturday I got the country station, and on Sunday mornings we would "Rise Up." We listened for the song of the day and then acted like teenage kids while calling and calling to try and be the ninth caller. We never won in the shop, but I'm pretty sure Kerry once won at home.

We laughed all day long, and when I say we laughed, we laughed so loud and hard they heard us all over that building. I'm sure it's very quiet in that building now.

When I broke the news to Kerry that I was going to close for sure, I could see the sadness in his eyes. I let him make the decision: we could close at the end of November 2019 or we could push on to the end of the year. He looked at me and said, "You love to make holiday cookies. Let's stay so we can do that one last time." So that became our plan. We made about 8,000 cookies—less than the approximate 12,000 cookies we normally would make, but I wanted nothing leftover.

We worked up until Christmas Eve and took the week after Christmas to clean out the space. Just like leaving Park Road, Tony mopped the floor for the last time. I taped my keys to the wall, and Kerry locked the door. Though both Tony and Kerry were sad, I was jumping up and down for joy.

This past year of 2020 has been just as hard on Kerry as it has been on everybody else. I pray that he finds a job after this pandemic and finds peace and happiness his life. I miss him so much.

I'm a little sad (okay the tears are running down my cheeks now) thinking of Kerry.

Kerry Lord and Sarah Bolton

THE YEAR WITH
NO HALLOWEEN

My work experience includes 25 years with the same retail company. I started as a sales associate, worked my way up to human resources, and then became the staffing manager. I also worked as an assistant manager of a Friendly's restaurant, went to culinary school, and took business courses at the local women's business center. I received my bakery experience from an awesome woman, Kim Foster, at Harvest Café and Bakery, where I got to know some of the inner workings of the field. It had always been my dream to open my own bakery, and I felt that my work and school experience were enough. But the knowledge I had could never prepare me enough for what was coming next.

It was a few days before Halloween of 2011. We were hit with an epic, downright ridiculous Nor'easter storm. Storm Alfred, better known as an "Oktoberblast," was a large low-pressure storm that brought on an unusually early snowfall. We had snowfall amounts that were 30-plus inches. I think all of us in Connecticut can tell you a story about that storm. It wasn't an ice storm, just a huge amount of that heavy wet snow; the flakes were about the size of a quarter. Downed trees and power lines left us with no power for days—weeks in some spots. Halloween had to be cancelled because people couldn't shovel out and had no power. Boy, people were so pissed! (See what happens when folks don't get their chocolate?)

At the shop we lost power for nine days. We lost all our perishable food, and I mean all! This included ingredients in the freezer and the walk-in refrigerator that were both in the basement. It was then that I found out I didn't have the proper liability insurance to cover all the damage. My insurance didn't cover loss of food because the storm was a natural disaster. Plus, I didn't have the correct writer for the loss of business revenue. And because the power line didn't come off the building, well, we weren't covered there either. Here I was, three weeks before Thanksgiving, and all the prep work that had been done was GONE, THROWN IN THE GARBAGE!

I did have an insurance agent, and he said when I took out my policy that I was all set. All set for what? Not for this. What a great time to find out that my policy didn't have what I needed. I asked the agent about this and these were his words: "Well, most people do not take it because it is more expensive." Really? Did you tell *me* about it? Did you give *me* the option to say no? I don't believe so. I was so beyond pissed. I remember sitting in my car at the Walmart parking lot screaming at the top of my lungs and banging my fists on the steering wheel. (Left me with some pretty nasty black and blue marks.) I couldn't comprehend what the insurance agent was telling me. I felt so stupid.

I could have turned off the lights, closed the door, and walked away right then and there— say, "To hell with all this shit. Screw everybody. Nobody thought I could make this work anyway." But I couldn't walk away, I just couldn't. There was that voice telling me everything would be okay.

THE MAN WITH
THE PLAN

We had just gotten our lights back on when I received a delivery of food. I had already made our prep lists, so everybody knew what we had to do to be able to pull off Thanksgiving. I didn't know how we were going to do it, but I moved forward like nothing happened, put myself in survival mode, and stayed there through the holidays. Everything was mapped out, and we were all on board to make this happen.

It was the beginning of the second week in November, on a Tuesday morning about 9 a.m., when a very well-dressed young man walked through the front door holding a leather-bound notebook. He had asked for me by my birth name, Elizabeth. Not very many people call me that, so it made the hair on the back of my neck stand up. He had come to sit with me and help me secure a Small Business Administration (SBA) loan to help me get through whatever it was that we had just been through. (Hell, I would say.) He seemed nice enough, so I thought, "I can do this."

Inside, I was happy to see some troops were sent in. I had screamed at everyone I could, so I think the insurance company figured they better send someone to keep me from jumping off a bridge or hurting somebody. As he was telling me about the process of applying for the loan, he asked me for my business plan. I said, "Excuse me?" as though my ears were filling with water and all I could hear was a swish swish sound. I told him that I didn't have any formal business plan. I thought his head was going to spin around; he just couldn't believe that I didn't have a business plan. And I had no answers.

He gave me until Thursday that week—two days (oh, and P.S., it was also two weeks before Thanksgiving)—to write and deliver my business plan. I was so angry that he had the nerve to ask me to sit down and write this business plan when I didn't even know all the legal jargon. I thought at least he could lend a helping hand in that department. I was knee-deep in Thanksgiving orders—300 pies and more! I knew he needed financial numbers, which I could provide for him, but the other stuff? Marketing, price comparison, core values, building my brand…I was at a disadvantage. I took the next day to look up business plans online and created a half-assed document. I was able to submit it and secured an SBA loan for $50,000. In total, I received $113,000 in financial assistance.

It's now 10 years later, and I can tell you that I have a business plan—a living document that I update every year. That young man for whom I held such deep anger, well, now I actually praise him. I should have been able to give him a business plan, or I should have at least had one done so that all I needed to do was tweak it for what I needed at that moment. The young man did me a favor by helping me realize just how unprepared I was.

So make damn sure you have a well-written business plan that is clear and concise, easily explainable to others, and recognizably yours. It's really not that hard; all you're doing is summarizing how you see your business. What it will look like? Who will be your customers? What will you sell? How much money do you intend to make? Will all the bills be paid? Don't let the fancy words get in your way of doing this. By creating a business plan, you'll get a good sense if you're ready or not. Do you have what it takes physically and emotionally? Opening a business isn't for the faint of heart.

I have created a workbook series called "Learning to Drive your Bus" that will become your road map for your business.

THE YEAR FROM HELL 2014

The bakery did well the next couple of years. We were doing more and more weddings and custom orders. Our schedule would get so filled that we'd have to stop taking cake orders; we could book up three to four weeks out. Some people would consider this a terrible problem. It made customers so mad that I just couldn't squeeze in that small six-inch cake or fulfill the "Oh yeah!" request to decorate the top like a wedding cake but with the special raspberry buttercream. Whew! We didn't complain though, because we knew those people just didn't understand that there was only so much we could do.

Holiday times were insane, but that's what I lived for. I loved the hustle and bustle of the holidays. Thanksgiving and Easter were my favorite. Truly though, seeing customers coming in time after time, meeting couples as they looked ahead to their special day…I felt honored to be a part of it all. We did retirements, baby showers, engagements, gender reveals, and just about any occasion that you would need a cake for. There were times people ordered a cake just because. There is a saying that life is too short to waste. To that I would add, "Eat the cake!"

I was feeling really good about what kind of community we had created. A Little Something Bakery had crossed the five-year mark and some people didn't think we would make it this far. We had our struggles, but I was showing all those nonbelievers that there was something special here.

I'm happy to tell you that by the end of 2013 we had $425,000 in gross sales. That was a LOT of cakes, cookies, cupcakes, pies, and other treats.

I wanted to hit that $500,000 mark so badly, but my labor costs were running at about 50 percent, which was way too high; they should've been around 30 percent. The price for food and materials was also rising. Some days I just shook my head at the price of butter or sugar. I did have to lay off some staff, which broke my heart. It was becoming difficult to manage all the bills and rent that had gone up. My stress level was increasing, and I just wasn't sure what to do. I turned to my accountant for advice. I was seriously thinking about closing the shop and creating an exit strategy. (Okay, I think I got up to 1,467 times I wanted to close this bakeshop ha-ha!)

Summertime was very slow in our town that year. It seemed like the carpet rolled up on Thursday nights and people didn't come back until Tuesday morning. I went to my landlord to see if I could get a reduction in rent or set up a payment plan that would help break up the rent and make it easier. At first he gave me a break. Then September 2014 came rolling around and I was served with eviction papers. (Actually, they were handed to one of my employees—and not even in an envelope!) I screamed and yelled and cried a lot this time. I was closing this place for good. I was given 90 days to be out. But once I thought about it, I realized this would at least take me through the holidays.

At the end of September 2014 we were at $483,000 in sales. Labor was taking up 50 percent, cost of goods sold was at 35 percent, which left only 15 percent for everything else. I hadn't received a paycheck and drew very little from withdrawals on owner's equity since I opened my shop. I was getting tired. I was defeated, but that voice in my head was still saying, "Nope, this is not the time."

Then came the beginning of October 2014 when I received a letter from my landlord's attorney stating that I needed to vacate the space by October 31 at midnight. How could they change the date like that? I did obtain legal counsel. He was a nice man; thoughtful and good. I wanted the opportunity to finish the year and the opportunity to reach $500,000 in gross sales. I knew we could certainly pass that amount. But after speaking with the attorney, he said rather frankly,

"Will you be any farther ahead if you stay?" I thought about it long and hard, and the truthful answer was no.

Then the landlord demanded some of my equipment be kept. I was so enraged. The attorney told me to just take my belongings and not make it any harder on myself and go. "Take the emotion out of it," he said. "Leave this behind and move on. Start fresh somewhere else and make people happy." (I wasn't sure what kind of advice that was since I was only moving two miles down the road.) But I was still concerned whether my customers would find me. To that he said, "This is just a business transaction."

How do you move on from your dream? How do you just call it a business transaction? How do you just close the door and turn the lights out?

We scrubbed that place and left it cleaner than we found it. The landlord kept one of my refrigerated cases and my dishwasher. See, he did huge business during the holidays and needed my space for his overflow of products. He needed the kitchen space for the prepared foods part of his business. Plus, he saw that we generated a lot of foot traffic and he wanted a piece of that pie. It was a calculated decision to have me move out earlier.

So here we were on Halloween, dragging our stuff out the door in the pouring rain. The shop was so bare and lonely. I didn't know how to take the emotion out of this one and just consider it a business transaction. I was leaving a community, one that supported us and loved us.

But I had already rented a new spot in an old industrial building at 485 New Park Avenue. I put those freakin' big girl panties on again, put one foot in front of the other, and off I went. This was the time to show everybody that I wasn't a quitter. Even though I wasn't leaving on my own terms, I was standing tall and proud! At least that's what I kept telling myself, not 100 percent believing it.

Inside 335 Park Road, West Hartford, CT.
It looked so lonely, like all the life had
been sucked right out!

485 NEW PARK AVENUE

It was such a strange feeling moving out of one space and into another. I wanted to go back and couldn't understand the complexity of what just happened.

The new space was 650 square feet. It was a box, I tell you, tiny in comparison to what I'd had before. It was four walls and a bathroom. But it was the only unit in this old building that had its own bathroom, so that meant it was special already! And the rent was cheap, so what more could I ask for?

We managed to get ourselves a refrigerator, oven, tables, and five (yes, I said five) sinks—and those sinks aren't cheap! For the life of me I couldn't figure out why each time the health inspector came in she wanted another sink. It annoyed me beyond belief. Five sinks? It actually made sense in the end, but I was still so frazzled and so sad from leaving Park Road, and she kept making such a big deal about these sinks. I just couldn't take it.

I really didn't know who we were anymore. Were we a bakery? Were we still A Little Something Bakery? It sure didn't feel like it. I tried to make it look like we were still on Park Road, but it wasn't the same. We didn't have nearly the same amount of space we had before. And where were all the people? There was no view to the outside, so I couldn't watch people walk by. All we had was a clouded-over skylight. We had some windows, but they faced the other side of the building. It was weird.

It didn't take me long to figure out that there was no foot traffic inside this building. It only had a few businesses in it, and they had their own distinct clientele. Getting the other business owners, let alone a customer, to travel into the dark hallway and up seven stairs was difficult, to say the least. Sure as hell though, you could smell our bakery the moment you walked in the main entrance. That sweet buttery aroma traveled its way into every crevice of that old building. People would walk around in circles trying to find where the smell was coming from. I think they were drunk on it and didn't take the time to read the signs pointing to where we were. It took a while, but soon the other tenants in the building came running in just to see what the aroma was.

As I was moving into my space, some other female entrepreneurs were also moving in. There were the ladies at Blaze and Bloom, an eclectic vintage shop. Jennifer, Katie, Tracy, and Julie were a great fit for the building.

Jennifer and I made fast friends and she was always there for a laugh or a cry—or for a glass of wine if we needed it. She is a true friend and a talented woman. I loved how she would come in for her cup of coffee each day she was in. She proudly took her cup off the rack, added some Splenda, and went to the fridge for the almond milk. She would take a couple sips, and it wouldn't be five minutes before she misplaced her coffee cup. You couldn't even play a joke on her by hiding her cup, she took care of that all by herself. I'm not sure she even likes coffee, but we still have coffee in the mornings via Face-Time. We share the real and raw look of just awaking for the day. We don't just tell each other what the other wants to hear; we tell each other the truth, no matter how brutal it may be. She's one of my trusted souls, and I love her with all my heart.

Rebecca Reinbold Couture owner Rebecca Reinbold and I became very good friends also. Her laughter and genuine concern for others makes her so special. Rebecca had her shop in the building for many years, and her entrance faced the outside in the back. Rebecca is a remarkable fashion designer; she makes made-to-measure clothing for all events. She specializes in wedding dress alterations and attire for bride and groom parties. With all the lace and bead work, the wedding dresses—along with the christening outfits she makes from them—are phenomenal! I would have to say that she's another one of my trusted souls. I love her so much!

I also met Amber Jones at the new location. Her specialty is empowering women through boudoir photography. Like Rebecca, Amber had a separate entrance from the outside of the building. Amber's work is incredible. This quote from her website says it all: "Our lives always seem to revolve around caring for someone other than ourselves. It is time to take a day to reconnect with your heart and soul and be reminded of the gorgeous, powerful woman that you are." Both Jennifer and Rebecca have done a session with her. I'm not there yet in my own personal growth to have a session.

At my son Christopher's wedding, Amber made sure I looked beautiful in the photos. Rebecca had altered my dress that I found at Panache, and Jennifer painted the Tardis doors that were used as the wedding backdrop. We held the rehearsal dinner at 485, and Christopher and his band set up in Jennifer's shop for a night of great music and fun.

Christopher and Sara's wedding cake.
There was a subtle "Dr. Who" theme.

I certainly don't want to forget Patti Dahle at Hello Dahle. Patti makes incredibly gorgeous custom decorative pillows for big-time designers, but she also has a small vintage shop where you can always find a quick gift or knickknack.

I was getting excited that there was a group of women in this building, and we had a great opportunity to share some of the same client base—if we all worked together. That's when I decided to rebrand and change our focus to the custom-made side of our business. We made and designed cakes, cupcakes, and cookies. Next to making cakes, I love making cookies. I didn't like making cupcakes, but they made up a third of my total sales so I had to like them.

It wasn't easy for customers to find me in the maze of the building even though I had signs up. I focused on social media and kept posting about the cakes and treats we made. The ladies in the building were so supportive and helpful. We actually helped each other. It was a great feeling to be a part of something that was so special. Eventually, we were able to attract quite a few customers and create a new presence on New Park Avenue.

The ladies of 485, as I like to call them, were an awesome group of women entrepreneurs. We were each at different stages of our business growth, but together we brought life to this old ball bearing building, built in 1903. There were so many neat nooks and crannies. I loved it when we had a holiday fair, when vendors lined the hallways with handmade goods. It was exciting to see people coming into the building and discovering all that was there.

During this time, I also met some wonderful businessmen. I came to know and respect Marvin Janow, a great man who owned the framing shop downstairs.

By the end of 2015, I just couldn't see how we could grow our business. We went from making $40,000 a month to making $60,000 for the whole year. Such a huge drop! Was it worth it? Would anybody ever find me in this building? And how do I get people to come into this building? That seemed to be a common thread among my fellow tenants. It was Marvin Janow who told me that I should make sure to give myself enough time to reestablish, that I hadn't given myself enough time in the building yet, to give it time and it will work.

Then there was Herb Jasper who owned Whamsco Kitchens right across the hallway. He was like the mailman; he never missed a day of work. At first, I couldn't get him to say much or even smile, but as time rolled on he would come in say hi and talk to us. Herb was a great neighbor.

I can't forget mention my very good friend, Dave Simonson. Dave worked in a part of the building that was down at the far end with an entrance on the outside. He worked at F3, a computer support and service company. Dave would take his daily stroll through the building and stop in to say hi. He is the kind of person who would do anything for you and not think twice. He has a heart of gold. We had many long conversations at my farm table. Dave liked to take care of all of us, he was that kind of person. He now lives in California, and because of him, I have a wonderful group of friends and a business coach out there. Dave's friendship is invaluable to me, and he is for sure my guardian angel. Where would I be without him?

A couple of years later, more women began opening up shops. Marguerite Rose ran Panache, a great consignment shop that she purchased from a previous owner and upgraded to an awesome little spot with such great finds. Marguerite has since moved to Park Road in West Hartford. Kim Greene owned a meditation studio turned vintage shop. Erica Moses opened Zona, a mid-century shop that was so bright and cheery! I loved that shop. She has now closed up shop in 485 but has an Etsy shop online. There was another photographer, Erica Stinziani, from Stella Blue. I had fun working with her on a few events and look forward to doing some work with her in the future. One of the last women to move in before I left was Susan Forrester. She was a lactation professional. I loved seeing all those babies go by my door. And there was Marvin's daughter, Laurel, who worked with him in the frame shop. She purchased the business when Marvin retired, though I still saw him a lot.

Another awesome group of women at 485 New Park was our knitting group. Someone had posted on Facebook (I'm not sure who) asking about a knitting group and wondering if there was one anywhere in town or if anyone wanted to start one. I replied right away and said I would love to host it in my shop. We met on Tuesday nights and were there to both knit and have a good time. We attracted a nice group of women: Amy Thompson, Stacey Willard (and sometimes her daughter, Charlotte), Rebecca Reinbold, and me. My mom, Toni Battistini, joined us for a while. Four of us met regularly since 2016— maybe 2015, I can't remember. If we were getting frustrated about something with our knitting, my mom would say, "Keep knitting!" We would laugh about it later, saying "Keep knitting!" OMG we would talk about everything; I don't think there is a subject we didn't touch upon.

And yes, we really did knit. Amy crochets the cutest baby blankets and animals, and she knits also. Stacey crochets and knits continental style, which means she knits superfast. She creates some of the prettiest shawls. Rebecca was working on a blanket, but many evenings she would do her hand-sewing. And then there's me. I'm the one in the group who knits but never seems

Photo by Amber Jones

to finish a project. It's not like I have never finished anything, but I do have a tendency to not like something halfway through and then change it up.

We've since moved our knitting group over to Rebecca's shop, since I no longer have a shop in the building. These women will tell you the good, the bad, and the ugly—whether you want to hear it or not—but they are the greatest friends. They are there for you when you need them.

There were a few other businesses at 485 New Park Avenue: Joe Cornfield Wallpaper;

Mobility One, a scooter and stairlift company, J & M Imaging, artwork reproduction, and high-resolution scanning; and WIP fitness studio. (I didn't go there; I would have died!) New Park Brewing came and made their new home in 485, which changed the demographics in the building. None of those customers would come down the hallway to see what wonderful businesses there were. The brewery is doing well, but after A Little Something Bakery closed and the COVID-19 pandemic hit, not many people were left in that building. So sad.

I really loved that building; it had so much potential. I remember the town newspaper wrote an article on the businesses at 485, which was such great press. We started getting a lot more foot traffic. People came and couldn't believe they drove by that building a thousand times and had no idea what was inside.

January 2016 through December 2019 were the best four years of owning A Little Something Bakery. Some of these ladies are still a part of my community. The circle is small, but the love is genuine. It gets no better than this.

Jennifer O'Connell, Rebecca Reinbold and me
at Christopher and Sara's wedding.
Photo taken by Amber Jones Photography 3/30/19.
This photo makes me smile every time I see it!

This past year of 2020 has been especially hard for me. I never thought in a million years that after I retired from baking, we would have a pandemic, and I would be at home all the time. There was nowhere to go, nothing to do, my business hadn't started as planned. At times the loneliness was really hard. Even to have a Zoom call with the ladies of 485 seemed like a huge mountain to climb. All I could do was find comfort in waiting for Tony to come home. I would sleep so much (talk about depression!). So glad it seems that the worst is over. Not sure what normal is, but I no longer feel trapped inside the house.

THE PURPOSE

It was late October 2019. I was sitting at the farm table in my bakeshop listening to a recording from my business coach, Caterina Rando. I was listening to her speak about getting ready for 2020 by setting our sales goals and, if needed, taking a look at things differently, making sure we had our strategies in place. In doing so, we should venture outside our boxes, step outside our comfort zones, and take risks. This kind of thinking, she said, will help you take your ideas and manifest them.

So, I casually looked around my shop. It was a box, a cube actually. This place had become my comfort zone. Every morning when I stepped over the threshold and into that space, my heart felt at ease. There was no life outside these four walls; it was a sanctuary for me. Taking a risk, well, I felt I had taken a lot of risks in the last 11 years. A feeling came over me; it was calm and peaceful. I wasn't sure if I should be nervous or not. I kept looking around my shop, but nobody else was there. A soft voice said to me, "It's time. You have accomplished all that was needed."

Time? Time for what? I sat for a bit longer and just looked around, taking in all that was there: my display of cake plates, the pictures on the wall of some of my favorite cakes I did for my customers, all my cake pans I had collected over the years, the array of vintage coffee mugs that hung on the pallet wood rack Tony had made for me…and my farm table. I thought about all that went on when we sat around that table. I thought about the couples who would come in and friends who stopped by. I had my first cup of coffee for the day there. Kerry and I ate lunch every day at that table. Jennifer would whisk on in, sit for five seconds, and off she would go again, forever looking for her coffee mug. When Amber couldn't get good Wi-Fi, she would come sit and do her work at that table. Ed would come meet his plumber friend and have a cup of coffee. Rebecca would pop in to say hi and see what I was baking because she could smell it in her shop. Patti always popped her head in during one of her walks around the building. Dave would stop in nearly every day just to see if we needed anything. He could add to the commotion on any given day; he was one of those silent "Who, me?" evils.

I decorated and packaged cookies at that table. It had grown to be more than just a farm table. It had become a symbol of who we, better yet, who *I* was. Kitchen tables are very important to me. Even today, my life revolves around the kitchen table. No matter what holiday, or any gathering for that matter, we always wind up at the table. In my house we sit for dinner together, no matter if it's two or more. We laugh, we cry, it's the central place in our home. That held true for my shop; the table was the central place in there. All were welcome to come to the table.

I took some time sitting there and thinking. I knew what I needed to do. See, since my shop was the "box," the space was my "comfort zone," and the risk would be to close the shop and walk out the door. I was just shown that I had accomplished so much, learned so much about people and baking and myself. I had met thousands of beautiful people and baked a lot of cakes, cupcakes, and cookies. I became very calm as a peacefulness wrapped around me like a warm blanket. I wasn't frightened but knew that I needed to go. The only way I could personally and professionally grow was to walk out that door. I needed to show the world everything I had learned.

I spoke with my daughter first. She helped me realize that my decision was made, and the path had been chosen. Even though I didn't know exactly where I would be going, this felt right. It had just hit me: I was left here to learn everything I needed to learn so I could help others. Boy, was I about to go on a journey.

My Farmtable

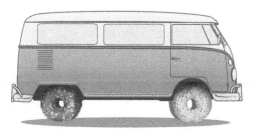

INGREDIENTS NEEDED
FOR A SUCCESSFUL
SMALL BUSINESS

What happened next would be the beginning of a slow revelation, and perhaps the greatest entrepreneurship lesson I've ever learned. It is this: Processes are good. I originally thought they'd stifle my creativity, but they do the exact opposite. They support creativity. Eventually, you have to step out of survival mode in order to thrive. It's the brutal truth of being a founder. Yes, LEAP. Yes, RUN. Yes, GET UP WHEN YOU GET KNOCKED DOWN AND TRY AGAIN. This is how you build a business. But once that business is built, and moving and growing, you're going to have to stop, reassess, and edit your methods. You have to find new ways to communicate, tell your team what you need, and to hear what they need. You have to learn to ask for (and give) help.

Building a business will always be a work in progress, and new processes will always be required as you grow. There's no one system that saves the day forever.

*But back then, I didn't know any of this.
Which is how I ended up throwing my team
into madness.*
– Ellen Bennett, Founder and CEO,
Hedley & Bennett[1]

I included this quote because it spoke to me about the exact mindset that you need to have when opening a business. It speaks directly to all of us who have a business or who want to start a business. As your business grows and changes, you must do the same also. You'll must keep in mind how we communicate with our team and let them know about decisions you are thinking about making or big jobs that you are about to undertake. A buy-in from your team is important so you can meet your business goals.

---

[1]Bennett, E. (2021, April 16). I built apron brand Hedley & Bennett into a fast success. Our lack of structure almost brought us to a halt. Entreprenuer.com. https://www.entrepreneur.com/article/368378

CHAPTER

UNDERSTANDING SMALL BUSINESS TAXES

Now, I'd like to think I have a brain in my head; but things were so crazy when we first opened, all I could think about was the baking and making sure we had enough cupcakes or almond clouds to fill the cases.

So, when the accountant asked me about necessary business items like taxes and whether I was putting money aside, I was like Damn! How was that to happen? How would I know how much to put aside?

I learned the hard way that this next part is very important. And it's not so scary once you get it together. Let's start by listing the different types of taxes you are responsible for: (Some of these apply only if you have employees, but you should still be informed.)

1. Federal Tax
2. Federal Withholding Tax
3. State Sales and Use Tax
4. State Withholding Tax
5. State Unemployment Tax
6. Federal Unemployment Tax
7. Business Entity Tax
8. Self-Employment Tax.

See, there's a lot to keep straight.

I'm pretty good at following directions; if I was told about these taxes, what they were and when they were due, I would have had this all written down with folders or binders for each. Actually, I like the whole organizing thing. But no one explained any of this to me. On the other hand, I thought I knew what I was doing. By me not knowing the correct information, it left me with a $56,000 IRS tax bill.

I was able to straighten out the state taxes and get them paid off much quicker. But the IRS bill is a civil penalty, so I have a payment plan in place. It's been reduced, but it's still there. They withhold my husband's tax return every year, which I don't think is fair. This penalty will be with me for a little while longer or until I reach out for an offer and compromise. So remember, just because you're an LLC doesn't mean you're not personally liable for monies owed to the government.

I guess by now you might be asking yourself why the hell I opened a business. Well, I really thought I knew what I was doing. But clearly, I could have taken a couple more steps early on to help me make this journey a less bumpy and a little more profitable.

Success starts with *one*. One step. One client. One order. One sale. Your business may not be where you want it to be right now, and that's okay. Don't give up. Continue to work hard and trust the process! That's my philosophy. I believed it then and I believe it now. I'm sure that if I had the right strategies in place from the beginning, I would have been able to handle some of my mistakes better—or not have had them at all.

BUILDING A BUSINESS PLAN

Many business owners make the mistake of creating a business plan because they were told to. They hop online, find a template, plop in some information, and POOF! they think they have a business plan. That isn't how it works.

Please make sure you take the time to do your homework first and understand why you're creating this document. The most effective small business plans are the ones that are used as living documents. They can help guide you in your decisions and keep your business on track.

I understand the excitement of opening a new business and wanting to just get into your spot and start working, but the planning stages MUST come first. You have to understand what you're doing. Yes, you'll have your foundation to help you, but you need to understand what parts you are responsible for.

Talk to any small business owner and you'll find that starting a business requires a lot of work. An idea doesn't turn into a business without adding some elbow grease. Some budding business owners understand the work necessary to start a business, but they might not be familiar with all the steps needed to launch a business. If you're willing to put in the hard work, you're going to want to know the best possible ways to reach your goals. Remember the quote from the beginning of Section 2.

Some people believe in taking a middle-of-the-road approach, recognizing that not all businesses need a comprehensive business plan. It's suggested though, to at least have a lean, simple business plan for startups that highlights the basics. Focus on the parts that make the most sense for your business. These are items that are important to include in your business plan:

1. **WHAT** do you want to achieve?
   This is part of your vision statement. It will describe to others your long-term goals for your business. They should be big and ambitious and should inspire you and your team. In a perfect world, what does your business look like?

2. **WHY** this business?
   This is part of your vision statement. Why is this business important to you? Why is now the time to start this business? Why do you wake up every day to do the things you do? For whom do you do this? For your business to survive, you need to stand out and thrive! This includes income, children, etc. In the words of Simon Sinek, "Always start with why. It's good to know why you are launching your business."

3. **HOW** will you achieve your goals?

This is your mission statement. It will tell people the purpose of your small business. A mission statement can be short and easy to remember, such as Nike's statement, "Just do it!" Mission statements often change as your business changes. You should include some financial numbers in your mission statement. How will you make this business profitable? It's also another way to hold yourself accountable for your goal, allowing you to assess your progress as you go.

When I opened A Little Something Bakery, it was my mission (my purpose) to make people happy with fresh, made- from-scratch baked goods, just like Grandma did.

4. **WHO** is you customer?

This is about your target market for your business. Not everybody is your customer. This part involves focusing on the best customer for *your* business. This is worth the time and effort you put into it.

As for me, I believed that everybody was my customer. I mean, who doesn't like yummy, home-made baked goods? But in fact, not everybody understands your product. Yes, that holds true for a bakery. I was quick to find people of my or older generations who appreciated what I was doing. This was total from-scratch baking; it didn't taste like it came from the grocery store or a box. Some generations of people only know the grocery store bakery. (Just thinking about the number of pre-servatives in those products—YUCK!)

People who grew up with strong ethnic back-grounds were also my customers because their family's beliefs were the same values that I have. Their kitchens were a big part of their family's lives, where everybody got together to help make a holiday meal or bake holiday cookies.

For example, I had a friend tell me a story about a time when he brought home a sour cream coffeecake from our shop and took it to his mom's house for a holiday. She took a bite and asked where he had gotten it. She's an excellent baker in her own right, but she was blown away with how incredible this coffeecake was. This was a good old-fashioned sour cream coffeecake with swirls of cinnamon and sugar. (It doesn't get any better than that.)

So, you'll want to know the characteristics of your ideal customers. Why do they need and want *your* product or service? Why should they do business with *you*? What kind of customer do you like to work with? Are your current customers your ideal customers?

5. Who is your **COMPETITION**?

   Knowing who your key competitors are and understanding their strengths and weaknesses is another way to determine who your clients are.

When I closed my shop, I had to tell my customers who I recommended they go to instead of me. I couldn't leave them hanging. I did contact two other bakeries that I believed could serve my customers well and had the same values as I did. I made sure that I knew what their products tasted like, and I made sure I understood their customer service. After I did my homework, I was ready to recommend the two places that I felt would be as close to mine without being me.

6. WHERE will your business be?
Will it be online only, or will you have a brick-and-mortar location? Where will it be located? Will customers be able to find you? Do YOU have a bus? What does it look like?

7. PRODUCTS & SERVICES
This is the part of your business plan where you describe the specific products or services you offer. You will fully explain how your products are made, along with how and where you buy your materials. Don't forget to add what kind of packaging you will have (if any).

8. PRICING
If you have a high-value, highly unique product or service, your offering may be more conducive to premium pricing, which lends itself to a different target market.

Remember my friend Rebecca? She's the fashion designer and dressmaker. She has a high-value, highly unique product. Her wedding dresses and other special occasion dresses are one-of-a-kind. Rebecca can charge premium pricing for what she does.

Make sure that when you're pricing your product or service you're charging enough money to cover your costs. You are in business to make a profit, after all.

Below is a good formula, so you should print it or write it down and keep it in a folder or binder. (I prefer binders.) I used to keep a binder with how much each "base" cake cost and then when we added decorations; it was easier to add that portion on. I kept a list of every item we made, that way if the price of material goods (like butter) went up, I could easily adjust. There are computer programs that will do this for you, choose whichever you prefer.

Material Costs

When you get your receipts, add up the money that went into making your product. If your supplies made more than one product, then you'll need to divide it up, so you have your per-item material cost. Make sure that you're using your resale tax number in purchasing the items.

Labor Costs

You'll need to set an hourly rate for your time (say $35.00/hour) and then how many products you can make per hour (say you made five). Divide your hourly rate by that number to find your labor cost per item. By no means pay yourself minimum wage; you and your product are worth more than that.

Delivery/Shipping

You'll need to calculate the price of delivery/shipping if you plan to offer it. Do NOT offer it for free. Compare local sources like USPS, FedEx, and UPS. Your customers are used to paying shipping fees by now.

Third-Party Market Fees

Please remember to include your merchant fees (Square, Stripe, PayPal, etc.) into the price of your product or service. It will be roughly 3 percent, which would equate to $1.20 on a $40.00 item.

Other Costs

There is a cost for the labels, packaging, and other items you'll need in your business. When you get the invoice in, you should be able to determine the price per item. The vendor will usually have that. If you aren't sure, take the price of a bundle of boxes, labels, or bags, and divide the total cost by the number of items you received.

9. MARKETING & ADVERTISING

In this section, you'll briefly discuss how you'll market your product or service. How will you let your clients know where you are? Will you have a website, email, social media accounts? Since marketing is a crucial step in launching and driving your business, it's important to set realistic budgets. Yes, you need to budget for marketing, just like you would budget for anything else such as your accounting, heating, and rent. What will you name your company? How far do you want your reach to go? Who needs to know about your business?

10. LIABILITY INSURANCE

Ask questions; don't assume anything when it comes to insurance—or anything else for that matter. It's your responsibility to know what kind of coverage you have on your cars and homes, and the same holds true for your business.

I did get some money for the replacement of food after the Halloween storm that we had. (I think because I screamed so loud, I scared a lot of people, or they thought that I was so bat-shit crazy, they had to do something). When I did get another insurance agent, I knew what questions to ask.

11

CHAPTER

ASKING QUESTIONS

*Lessons learned is the knowledge gained
from the process, this includes the positives
and the negatives.
The idea is not to repeat the mistakes.*
– Author Unknown

So now that you know what to include in your
business plan, let me share with you the questions I ask my clients to see if they're ready to start
on their own journey:

- Do you have the skills for the job?
- What experience do you have that will help you open this business?
- Besides the foundation I speak of, who else will you need? (It's really like applying for a job, but this time you're the employer and the employee.)
- To what extent is your knowledge about the journey you're about to embark on?
- Where does your expertise lie?
- What sort of life do you want?

These are all questions you should have the answers to. They may not seem important, but if you're hopping on that bus and into the driver's seat, you'll need to organize your thoughts and put them on paper; this is your road map. Many new entrepreneurs feel as though this step can be skipped. I'm here to tell you it shouldn't. There are many benefits to having a business plan, both for your business and for you as an entrepreneur.

For me, when I opened my bakery, it was during some of the worst economic times that our country had yet seen. I felt I needed to take a step back and see what I might have been missing. I knew I had an excellent product and believed that by opening an old-fashioned bakery I could take us all back to a time when life wasn't so crazy. When times seemed simpler, there were no cell phones attached to everybody's ears. And what happened to respect and kindness? I wanted that piece of the pie back.

I thought of how I grew up in the late '60s and '70s. At A Little Something Bakery we were able to achieve that feeling and more. It was remarkable to watch as our community grew and we increased our following. I wasn't the only person who was nostalgic; there were others who felt the same way I did. We had become known as just "Little Something" or "The Bakery."

With that in mind, here are my answers to some of the previous questions:

- Do you have the skills for the job?
  I'm a great baker; it's what I've loved to do for a long time. But as you've seen, I was missing some expertise in certain parts of my business. Now I can tell you with 100 percent certainty

that I do have expertise in running a small business, understanding business tax structure, and knowing the importance of who and when to pay.

I've become an expert in bookkeeping after receiving my QuickBooks® certification. I completely understand labor costs, cost of goods sold (COGS), and operational expenses. Payroll…well let's just say I now understand all facets of payroll for a small business.

I also know now what it's like to have a good team in place. At the end, I realized what that really meant. I understand marketing, but that isn't my field of expertise, and I'm not very good with technology. What do I do about that? I've found people to assist me in those areas. I no longer feel as though I need to do everything myself. The things I don't completely understand or don't want to do I let somebody else handle for me.

- Besides the foundation that I speak of, who else will you need?

The people I need to help me run my business include the following:

An Accountant
Make sure you're both on the same page! Make sure they're there to help you, not just to do your taxes at the end of the year.

A Banker
Find someone who can help you get your bank accounts set up who will also be there to help you with financial questions. A financial planner is a good resource also.

An insurance Agent
I like to use an agent instead of going right to a company. Agents can compare companies and prices to ensure that you have the proper coverage for your business.

A Lawyer
This person is here for legal advice. Some people prefer websites such as LegalZoom. I personally want to see and speak with the person I'm dealing with.

- What sort of life do you want?

I've worked at warp speed for over 11 years. I was always too tired to enjoy the holidays because I busted my butt to make everybody else's holiday a good one, including when I was in retail. I realize now that working the way I did wasn't the smartest way to work. As I move into my 60s, I still want to work, just not so damn hard. The food industry is a killer, and it's not something I'd want to do again. Don't get me wrong, I loved what I did, and I loved my bakery. But as a small business owner there is no day off. You work around the clock, 365 days a year. I do believe that every working person should do a stint in food service; then, and only then, will they appreciate the work that goes into making your food. Some days I miss baking, but not enough to jump back into the fire.

I want to have a career where I really can make a difference in somebody's life; it's a calling. This path has been chosen, and I'm happy to drive down it and see where it takes me. I've got blind faith, I guess. I want to spend more time with my husband and my family. There were so many holidays that I just couldn't even stay awake for dinner; Christmas was the worst for me. I'll have the opportunity to spend more time at the beach—the sanctuary to my soul. I'll make sure that we have enough money to get the bills paid and have some extra for us. I plan on being around for a while and there's so much more living to do, so many people to help. I'm totally up for this journey.

Today, I don't have to focus on the amount of capital needed as I did when I opened the bakery. I'm working from home, and a couple of days a week I help a friend out at her co-working space. It's a nice change of scenery. There's no overhead. I do have a long-range plan, no funding required. This time around I'm not starting from scratch; I'm starting with experience.

HAVING
A BUSINESS COACH
(BING, BING, BING!)

*Caterina Rando is the founder of
the **Thriving Women in Business
Community**. She is on a mission to teach,
mentor and support women to be themselves,
do their thing, serve their people and
massively monetize their mastery. She shows
women entrepreneurs how to be loud and
proud about the value they bring in order
to make their businesses thrive. Her clients*

grow, shine, expand, open themselves up to new possibilities and take their businesses further then ever before. **Caterina is all about, positivity, integrity, generosity, community, providing and massive value while uplifting others**.
www.twibc.com

A business coach can assist and guide you, the business owner, in running a business. They do this by helping you achieve clarity about your business and determining how it will fit with your personal goals. Business coaching is a process used to take businesses from where they are now to where the business owner wants to be.

My business coach is Caterina Rando. It only takes one conversation with Caterina to feel her energy through the phone. She's amazing to talk to or be with on a Zoom call. My friend, Dave, who now lives in California, is a friend of Caterina. He gifted me her coaching services toward the end of 2018. I was honored to be working with her.

She has a personality that's bold and vivacious. Even through a Zoom call she commands presence when she's in the room.

Caterina's signature saying is "Bing, Bing, Bing!" It's used to celebrate and show support when one of the ladies has done something to move themselves forward, either in their business or on a personal level. The first time you hear it, you just sit there and say, "What the Hell?" I did everything I could to stifle my laugh, but she always sees me laughing. (I'm like the kid who got caught with their hand in the cookie jar.) You should have seen my husband's face the first time he heard it—he laughed his ass off.

I love Caterina and everything that she stands for. I just completed The Shiro Summit, a weekend seminar with her and a lot of other amazing women who are in The Thriving Women's Business Community. I wish I could list them all, but that list would be way too long. These women come mainly from the West Coast, but some of us are in different parts of the country. I still have to use my fingers to figure out the time difference, LOL!

A business coach can be your trusted soul when it comes to your business or anything else going on in your life. They are the one who pushes you if you need pushing, but they are also the one who will hug you if you need a hug. (Though during this year of COVID-19 we haven't been doing a lot of hugging.) Caterina has taught me that I need to get out of my own way, stop trying to make everything perfect, and realize that nothing *is* perfect. That's really hard for me, even today as I sit here and write this book.

She had me go through her "Thrive at Sales" class two and a half times. Halfway through the third time I finally called her on the phone and said I need to stop. There are things in my life that are far more important than trying to sell right now in the middle of a pandemic. I was so depressed and lonely. The year 2020 was very isolating, and the last thing I could think of was trying to sell myself to somebody when I had no idea who I was. I think then Caterina began to get to know the real me. I can do a great job of hiding what I don't want other people to see.

I did everything in my power to hide all my feelings during 2020.

I've never met Caterina or any of the wonderful friends I have made in California in person, but I have grown to love them through Zoom calls. I told them all that one day I'll get to travel to California and meet them in person, and there will be a lot of hugging. But I won't be going on a cruise—YUCK! A large floating petri dish.

Caterina has taught me to embrace boldness, be visible, create value, and most importantly, be consistent. If it wasn't for her and the other ladies, I wouldn't be where I am today. They all helped me realize that I do have massive value. To put myself out there and show the world who I am, I don't need to be perfect. (Notice the *perfect* thing is coming up again.)

I'm very happy to have Caterina in my corner. Her knowledge and enthusiasm are over the top. I need someone like Caterina in my life so I can take what I've learned and help others. I no longer feel like I'm hanging on a limb waiting for it to break. I'm on the ground with my tribe and making things happen. That's how we get things done. I'm here to build a community, build trust, and make connections. If my thoughts and beliefs do not mesh with yours, well, that's perfectly okay with me. It doesn't mean I can't be your friend, it just means that you won't be one of the people who help me achieve happiness in my amazing new journey.

Thank you, Caterina Rando, for who you are and what you do. You've helped me become a better businesswoman, and I'm beyond excited to be driving my bus down my new path. I couldn't have done it without you. BING, BING, BING!

TAKING MY NEW JOURNEY

*Gratitude. It's a word to express thankfulness
and praise. It refers to the quality of
being thankful and the readiness to show
appreciation and return kindness.
I'm grateful for all that I have.*
– Beth Bolton

As I sit here at my dining room table, early
on Thanksgiving morning 2020, the year

of the global pandemic (turning 60 years old in this year sucked! I really wanted that 60th birthday party), I'm reflecting back on this year. Some people might say that they don't have anything to be grateful for. They may have lost their job, fallen ill to the virus, or lost a loved one to this virus. But for me it was a year of understanding my "WHY."

The direction was already given to me, but at first, I didn't know what kind of journey I was put on. I had an idea, but it was so much more than I thought. I had to ask myself how to be authentic. How do people get to know who I am? All the pieces began to fall into place.

I have fully accepted my journey and I know my "WHY." I'm here because I love helping women who are looking to follow their dreams. I want to give them the motivation and opportunity to discover their purpose and their passion. I want to help them drive and be there for them when there is a rough patch.

So, I'll be there to assist you in making decisions and remembering the value you have to give. Listen to your own voice. Too many people listen to the noise of the world instead of themselves. Look deep down inside. You know what you want and why. Let no one decide that for you.

I did receive a text just the other day from my adult daughter, Sarah. She said "It's interesting this year of 2020 with COVID. Many people say this year has sucked, it's awful, they want it to be over. But it's been one of my favorite years. I've done so much self-discovery, self-growth, weight loss, and health improvements and I found Luis who makes me so happy!" As a mom, how could I read that and not think, you're right! Even within the storm there are always good things. We're just focused on what the storm is and forget about what is close to home, right in front of us. My reply to my daughter was, "That is because there will always be Phoenixes that rise out of the ashes. It's never all gloom and doom. You, my daughter, are one amazing young woman and there won't be anybody or anything that will ever stand in your way. You make your mother proud with all that you have done so far in your life and all that you will continue to do. I love you more than you will ever know."

We didn't grow up rich, but rather poor in today's standards. I really didn't know any better until I turned 16 and got a seasonal job at the local mall for a major retailer. The manager of the department I was working in took me aside the day before Christmas and said that I wouldn't be kept on past the Christmas holiday—not because I wasn't a good worker, but because I didn't have the proper clothes for the job. It was then and there that I realized we were poor. It was the first time in my life I realized that there were haves and have nots. I would give my mom most of my paycheck, and I never questioned it. One of my teachers in school called the store and spoke with the HR manager at the time, and they helped me get some of the proper clothing so I could return to work. I went back to work for that same major retailer and stayed there for 25 years. I started as a sales associate and worked my way up to HR as a trainer, then an assistant HR manager, and then became the staffing manager.

I still think back and remember the incredible people I met. And you know that manager who told me about my clothes? She crossed my path years later when she returned to work in that store. I'm grateful that I didn't back down but found a way to get what I wanted.

I'm grateful today for all that I have. We're still not rich, but I've made decisions in recent years that have nothing to do with money. When I realized that not everything is based on money, my mindset changed. Financially we became more secure. Funny how by just changing your thought process and accepting responsibility for everything that happens to you—both the good and the bad—and by not allowing outside forces to drive your decisions, you become the one and only driver of your bus. Look for me. I'll be out on the road.

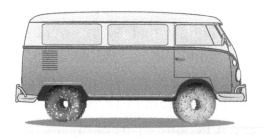

OH, BY THE WAY

As we end the year 2020 and usher in 2021, I've realized that saying goodbye to my bakery was much harder than I ever thought it would be. It was like a part of me was left behind, first on Park Road and then at 485 New Park Avenue. I thought leaving on my terms would be so much easier. There I was, jumping up and down for joy when I closed and Kerry locked the door for the last time. I was so excited to run, hop on my bus, and travel down my new path. I couldn't wait to help everybody who needed my help.

It's been a year now, a year that none of us expected. I thought my life would be so different by now; I thought that all my workbooks and workshops would be up and running. But that didn't happen. I had poured my heart and soul into A Little Something Bakery. It identified who I was, and it became a part of my life that I don't ever want to forget. I was so proud of everything that I accomplished, even though I was knocked off the road a couple times.

In the end, we did have to declare bankruptcy and take care of some tidying up to dissolve the business, a business transaction they say. I procrastinated like none other on this process, feeling that it would make everything so final. As I look back at 2020, I was trying to find a way to say goodbye and I just couldn't. Rather, I didn't want to.

I want to go back knowing what I know now. I want to smell that sweet buttery smell and see the customers walk through the door to get their morning coffee and treats. I want to see the kids rush in and press their faces up against the glass trying to decide what they wanted. I want to make the cakes for all the couples getting married. I want it ALL!

HOLD PLEASE!

I can't go back; I can only go forward. I must look out the front windshield and remember not to forget to look to the sides—there's no time for looking in the rearview mirror. I don't want to miss anything; I want to see it all. This is the path that I'm meant to be on. I'm happy to be on this journey, happy I could share this experience with you, and excited to know that I can help others bring their dreams to fruition. I hope to see all of you in 2021. I'm hoping to meet some of the friends I made via Zoom and in person and give awkward hugs to everyone I know.

Thank you from the bottom my heart.

Beth

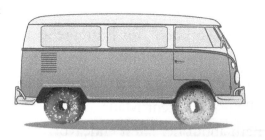

AN INTERVIEW WITH THE AUTHOR

ENTREPRENEUR COACH PROVIDES TOOLS FOR WOMEN BUSINESS OWNERS

Connecticut entrepreneur Beth Bolton knows her way around the kitchen—and the ins and outs of business ownership.

In late 2019, she retired from baking and launched Beth Bolton Coaching. She recently created a new series, Driving

My Bus: A Workbook for Entrepreneurs, to help female entrepreneurs build a strong foundation and guide them along their journey. MetroHartford Alliance Content Manager Nan Price spoke with Beth about her latest endeavor:

NAN PRICE: Tell us about your coaching business evolution.

BETH BOLTON: After I closed, I took the whole month of January 2020 to essentially adjust to my new life. During that time, I had some ideas about what I wanted to do—and I knew what my path was. I knew I wanted to help women in business, and I knew the best way I could teach them was through my own experience.

I have 25 years of retail experience. I had some restaurant experience, and then I obviously had my bakery. Yes, we had many misfortunes, but I wanted to be able to take those misfortunes and use them to teach women that they can have profitable and successful businesses if they're able to be proactive.

NAN: Why are women business owners your niche?

BETH: I chose women because they often have limited beliefs that they can be successful or profitable and others consider what they do as a hobby. I want to empower them to step outside the box and leave their comfort zones. You might be making handbags or jewelry and you're crushing it, but if you're not giving yourself goals and you're not trying to achieve goals, your business isn't going to grow.

I want to show women that, no matter what you're doing, you can set personal and financial goals—and then I want to provide them with the steps to achieve those goals.

NAN: Is that the premise of the workbook?

BETH: I first developed a one-pager *Are You Ready to Travel?* And I used a bus analogy that the four wheels on our bus are your foundation. My belief is that those four wheels should be a banker, a lawyer, an insurance advisor, and an accountant, and everybody else is a rider on your bus.

The one-pager is to encourage business owners to go through the thought process. The first question is: What is your passion? Aside from the monetary gain, I want you to really think about *why* you're opening this business. That really makes people stop and think. Once they know their passion and why they're doing what they're doing, the next step is to look at your vision. Where do you see your business going?

After I developed that one-pager, I realized I needed to take people to the next step, because they now know whether they're ready to move forward. So, I developed the workbook, which is also a template for a simple business plan. This isn't creating any big financial statement. It's just something to give them confidence and get them thinking about the business end of things.

NAN: How many women are you working with?

BETH: I'm working with about 10. Many are local, and a couple are on the West Coast.

NAN: How did you get them engaged in your process?

BETH: That's the hard thing. I took my experience and the connections I had while I had the bakery and reached out to people I know. I asked them if they were interested and if they wanted to attend my *Are You Ready to Travel?* workshop. From there, I asked if they wanted to come and do the *Driving My Bus* workshop.

NAN: Is the workshop primarily targeted toward people who are just starting or are you working with them along the growth phases?

BETH: That's a good question. It's phase one, early entrepreneurship. However, I'm finding women coming to me who are dealing with COVID-19. People who didn't know how to pivot.

NAN: For many, COVID-19 in business ownership is almost synonymous with pivoting.

BETH: Right. So, women whose shops have closed or feel stuck. We look at what else they can be doing.

NAN: So, you're really helping people with the question of What now or what next? What's next for you? Will you continue to coach women business owners through the next phase or put out another workbook?

BETH: I am going to put out another workbook. But first my focus is to finish writing my book—it's not a memoir. It really is an entrepreneur's journey.

NAN: I can't wait to read it!

BETH: I'm excited.

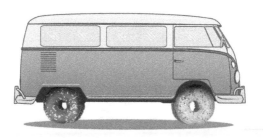

LEARN MORE ABOUT BETH BOLTON CONSULTING

www.bethbolton.com | Facebook | Instagram

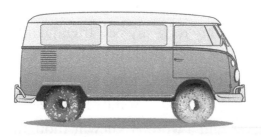

ACKNOWLEDGMENTS

Anyone can give up; it's the easiest thing to do. But to hold it together when everyone else would understand if you fall apart, well that's true strength.

There are so many people I'm grateful for who were with me for some part of my journey. You have to admit, there was a lot of laughter, crazy people, and big, huge messes in the kitchen. But there was a higher power controlling the direction I was heading in, and without you all the journey would have been a little rougher.

Tony Bolton: Where would I be without you? You drive me crazy, but I drive you crazy, so we're even. You're my rock, my best friend, and the best husband anybody could ever ask for. You proudly walked this complete journey with me, sometimes not approving of some of my decisions, but you never said a word (I knew it though). I look forward to us being able to spend more time together and getting to travel a little bit. We, as a couple, still have a lot more living to do.

Both my children, Christopher and Sarah: Had it not been for the two of you telling me to follow my dream, I might not have ever started on this journey. I remember the night at the dinner table when I told you about my plan. You both reminded me that I always told you to make sure you follow your dreams and never give up. Well, I listened. Now I want you to go make *your* dreams come true. Thank you!

Christopher Bolton: Thank you for being you and always showing your pride of A Little Something Bakery, and for the endless times you had to fix my computer (but only twice did melted butter get spilled on it). Then there's my phone—something is always going wrong. You helped me with the deliveries, putting food downstairs, and packing Bill's cookie order every year. It was some fun times. Thank you for marrying Sara, who came and helped with cookies and whatever else needed to be done toward the end when we were at 485. Thank you for taking those early shifts so I could sleep in a bit. You made sure I was taking a break and you always made sure I had my coffee. Your love and support have always been so much appreciated and there were some days I couldn't have done it without you. I love you!

Sarah Bolton: Thank you for your support. Not only did you help bake, but your moral support was unwavering. You always knew when I needed you without me even asking. Sometimes I just needed you there to keep me from freaking out. You made sure I ate, had my water, and sat down to take a break. I can't forget the delivery of that wedding cake with Daddy—having to climb up stairs to put a five-tiered carrot cake (so heavy) on a stage. Glad I was in a different part of the state for that one. A mother could not ask any more from a daughter. I love you!

Allison Reis, Nicole Edlund, and Rachael Edlund: Thank you for who you are and for all the hard work, love, and support you put into my dream. I'm so proud of you ladies.

Antoinette Battistini: Mom, thank you for supporting my dream and coming in to help work the front counter. Your time spent in the bakery was much appreciated.

Peter Edlund: I want to thank you from the bottom of my heart for the times you came to Connecticut from New York City to help work in the bakery and make holiday cookies. You've always been a huge supporter of the bakery and for that I greatly appreciate all your hard work. I love you and Todd Martin!

Karen and Cesar Reis: Your pride and love for my bakery meant so much to me. You two always made me feel good about my decision to open up my shop. We must continue our get-togethers! Is it time for wine yet?

Jason Reis (and Connie): I know you two didn't live close enough to be with us a lot, but your love from afar was certainly felt.

Paul Edlund: Thank you for bringing your girls to the bakery and picking them up when they were done with work. Your love and support always made me smile. I think I know as many people in town as you do. LOL!

Jennifer and Dan Grace: I want to thank you for your support of my dream. I know that you didn't get to spend as much time inside the bakery as the others, but you had two little ones and you lived far enough away that you just couldn't hop in the car and drive up.

Stanley Kasparewicz and Leslie Lerner: Thank you for your support. Uncle Stan, that countertop is still in use today.

Kerry Michael Lord: Thank you for who you are and all you did to make our last three years successful.

Thank you to the following people who loved and supported A Little Something Bakery. Each and every one of you has contributed to the success of our little community:

Nancy Sullivan: Thank you, my dear friend, for traveling with me on my journey. I have known you for a long time and I love you!

Kathy Horner the late Don Horner: You both always believed in me and my dream. Don Horner, I miss you so much.

Melanie Ceccarelli: My friend, all I have to say is "pasta dinner" and we all smile! I thank you for everything you did to help me.

Joyce (Kucia) Leone and Mark: Thank you for the support you have always given to the bakery and me. Joyce, you are my oldest friend of 55 years—WOW! I love you!

Kim Pita: My friend, thank you for all your support.

Jacob and Alli Studenroth: It all started with some cupcakes for Miss Porter's School. Then some wedding cookies. But I have to say that Henry's first birthday cake was EPIC!

Mike Keo and Chengyeng Lor: You are two people who I watched grow into one incredible couple with two amazing children.

Gregory Shimer and the late Tracey Gamer-Fanning, with a tear in my eye, I want to thank you. I got to watch the two of you become one. I know that we all will never forget Tracey, but Greg, I also know that you will help continue her work. Thinking of you makes me think of her. I can only smile for having the chance to have met two special people and being a part of your special day.

Amy Kidd: ROLL TIDE ROLL, my Alabama girl! I love you so much. Thank you for who you are and what you did for me.

Kim Foster: You are where it all began. Thank you for the opportunity to show what I was capable of doing. I love you!

Jennifer O'Connell: My friend, my world would not be the same without you.

Amber Jones: My friend, I'm so glad that I met you and have the opportunity to see what a phenomenal photographer you are.

Rebecca Reinbold: My friend, words cannot express how much I miss you every day!

Amy Thompson and Stacey Willard: Thank you for helping me get through some of the rough stuff and for making us laugh so hard at knitting. I miss you.

Helen Lee: I look for you every time I see the Animal Control van!

Tracy Barrett Flater: My partner in crime on Park Road.

Nan Price: You have played such an important role in my business life. I'm so glad I can call you friend also!

Dave Simonsen: You are my guardian angel; you hold a part of my heart. I thank you for everything that you have done for me. I look forward to seeing you when I make it to the West Coast.

Ned Davidson: Thank you from the bottom of my heart for your words of wisdom and the time you took out of your busy schedule. I heard you talking to me so much in the end.

Fizzy Memories: Thank you for the use of WANDA. I'll soon have my own bus; she will be named ALICE.

Nicole Bedard: Thank you for being my brand photographer and all the great photos you take. Thank you for finding WANDA.

Melina Erwin and staff @ THE ENTREPRE-NEURIAL CENTER-WOMEN'S BUSINESS CENTER, UNIVERSITY OF HARTFORD.

Caterina Rando: *The Thriving Women in Business Community.*

Annisa Teich: Owner of The Small Business Collective and West Hartford Coworking.

Thank you, my friend for helping me get to where I am today. Your love and support are so special to me.

The team that helped me put this book together:

Edited by: Nancy Graham-Tillman
Cover design by: Nelly Murariu
Back cover by: Marlene Kurban
Typeset by: Medlar Publishing Solutions Pvt Ltd., India
Jenn T. Grace: PYP Academy Press: Thank you for all your support and being my trusted soul through this process. I am forever grateful!

I know I'm forgetting others; I apologize.

To each and every customer who walked through the doors of A Little Something Bakery, whether we were on Park Road or on New Park Avenue. I thank you for your support.

To everybody who entrusted us to make cakes, cupcakes, or cookies for your special event. Thank you for your support. I've learned so much about our community. I'm so glad that I live here, but prouder that I created a little slice of heaven in A Little Something Bakery.

Enjoy life. Eat Cake.

Beth

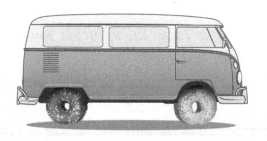

PRAISE FOR
THE BAKERY

After 25 years of working as a retail executive for the May Department Store, Macy's, and G. Fox & Company, Beth Bolton decided it was time to launch a second career. She had always dreamed about owning a bakery/coffee shop, but the truth was that her knowledge of the industry was limited, and she needed to learn more about the full range of bakery products before undertaking such an endeavor.

Could she do it? Her impetus came from her children who supported and encouraged her to follow her dream so that later in her life she wouldn't have to ask herself, "what if"?

With her support system in place, she challenged herself to fully understand the full range of bakery products as well as the nuts and bolts of owning and operating a bakery. Beth enrolled in the Connecticut Culinary Institute and got a job working at a bakery in Simsbury, which gave her the confidence and experience to bring her dream to fruition. And after noticing an empty storefront on Park Road in West Hartford many times, she decided that this was the perfect location for her business.

Beth opened her bakery in 2009 at the height of the Great Recession but nevertheless managed to build a customer base. She also reached out for help with payroll, state and employment taxes, and other variables she couldn't control. Then after two years in business, disaster struck when Storm Alfred paid a visit in 2011 and the bakery was without power for nine days just three weeks before the busy Thanksgiving holiday. Luckily, The Small Business Admininstration disaster team was sent to Connecticut in response to the hurricane, and Beth received an SBA disaster loan to help maintain operations.

At about the same time, Beth called SBA Lender Relations Specialist Bill Tierney to discuss cash flow issues. Bill put her in touch with HEDCO, a Connecticut-based SBA micro lender, that not only assisted with technical questions but ultimately lent the business $113,000 to purchase equipment for the bakery.

Despite all the adversity, A Little Something Bakery continues to operate because of its high-quality products and the fact that it offers "a little something" in addition to excellent baked goods to each of its customers.

Another strength is that Beth is committed to training her nine employees on every facet of the business such as counting money, giving excellent customer service, achieving daily goals, creating new products, being resourceful, and avoiding waste. The cost of supplies has risen almost 100 percent since she opened the doors, so she wants her employees to be diligent about production costs.

Beth believes in asking for help and has been counseled by the West Hartford SCORE Chapter and the Women's Business Center where she is in the process of rewriting her business plan. She recently joined the Park Road Business Association to increase networking opportunities.[2]

I have a sweet tooth. Actually, based on how much I like sugary items, it's more likely that I have a whole mouth of sweet teeth. So recently when I was driving down Park Road in West Hartford and saw that a new bakery opened next to Hall's Market, I just had to stop in and check it out.

I was happily greeted by the owner, pastry chef and West Hartford resident Beth Bolton and a co-worker, as they waited on a few other customers. I took my time making my selections as I looked beneath the little glass domes that carefully housed delectables. Oh, the choices! Should I go with the Lemon Blueberry Scone, a Blueberry Muffin, or maybe a Crumb Cake Square? The shop smelled heavenly, so I figured I really couldn't go wrong, no matter what I decided.

The Dirtbomb won my first pick—a mix between a donut and muffin, covered in sugar spice goodness.

---

[2]US Small Business Administration. (n.d.). A Little Something Bakery, West Hartford, CT. sba.gov. https://www.sba.gov/offices/district/ct/hartford/success-stories/little-something-bakery-west-hartford-ct

I also chose a Raspberry Breakfast Bar, a more traditional treat with a shortbread-like base, raspberry jam middle layer, and butter crumb topping. Both were presented nicely and traveled well back to my home in their cardboard bakery box.

The Dirtbomb did not disappoint. It was happily noshed with some milk. I also had a tiny piece of the oversized Raspberry Breakfast Bar, which was also quite tasty.

A Little Something Bakery offers pies, tarts, cakes, cookies, and cheesecakes, in addition to their breakfast treats. They also help plan items for other special events, including wedding cakes.

So, if you're in the Park Road area and have a hankering for something sweet, be sure to stop by A Little Something Bakery.[3]

[3]A Little Something Bakery—West Hartford. (2009, February 26). NBCConnecticut.com. https://www.nbcconnecticut.com/local/ghreb-a-little-something-bakery-west-hartford/1862541/

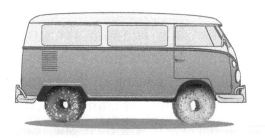

ABOUT THE AUTHOR

Elizabeth (Beth Ann or Beth) Edlund Bolton is one of five children born to the late Robert C. Edlund and Antoinette (Toni) Kasparewicz Battistini. Beth is the second oldest child. They spent their early years growing up in Canton, CT., until they moved to West Hartford, CT when Beth was about 12 years old.

Beth enjoys listening to music, reading, knitting, and being at the beach, let's not forget that glass of wine!

Beth has always had a passion for baking. As she got older and had children of her own, she had the opportunity to bake more. She started her side hustle while she was working full time at a major retailer. After attending The Connecticut Culinary Institute focusing on Pastry and Baking, Beth took her first leap of faith and went to work for a small bakery, It was there she realized that she wanted her own bakery.

As you read through this book you will see how Beth's passion grew and all that she accomplished while owning A Little Something Bakery.

Beth now works to assist women in making their dream and passion come true. She starts you out to make sure you have a strong foundation to succeed. You will see how passionate she is about what she is doing. While you are out there traveling along your journey, make sure you make Beth Bolton one of your stops along the way.

Top left-bottom right:

Groom's Cake ("Dr.Who" theme), "This is Us" five siblings and Todd, Tony and me, Peter and me, Christopher, Christopher and his Sara, Wedding Cake, Grandma and my nephew Noah, My Sarah and Kerry Michael Lord. Yes, I made the cakes and Kerry did the decorations.